To:
Stefan & Savion
June 3, 2006

MW00679325

Mikki's Choice

For my nephew, Dev,
Hard work pays off

Text copyright © 2005 by Carmel S. Victor
Illustrations copyright © 2006 by Angelina Winfield

Requests for permission to make copies of any part of the work should be mailed to the following address: Lemrac Books/Permissions, PO Box 541, Stockbridge, Georgia, 30281

www.lemracbooks.com

Library of Congress Cataloging-in-Publication Data
Victor, Carmel S.
Mikki's Choice / Carmel S. Victor: with illustrations
by Angelina Winfield

Summary: A lot has happened since Mikki became a new member of the family. After Mr. Thomas makes a surprising discovery about Mikki, the kids have to make a difficult decision. The surprise continues, as Mikki himself helps them decide his future.

ISBN-10: 0-9763078-1-2
ISBN-13: 978-0-97630-781-5

Printed in the United States of America

Mikki's Choice

Written by Carmel S. Victor

Illustrated by Angelina Winfield
Lemrac Books

iv

Chapter 1

One day there was a big change at home. Papa came to tell us he was getting a German Shepherd Puppy from an animal shelter.

He told us German Shepherds were nice dogs.

We were all excited, and decided to set up a Welcome Puppy Club.

✔ My brother, Darryl- 9 years old.

✔ My sister Dominique- 6 years old.

✔ Our twin cousins who came to spend the week-end with us, Corina and Corey- 4 years old.

✔ Jessica, their older sister- 7 years old.

✔ Little Mike, a neighborhood kid, also, Darryl's best friend- 8 years old.

✔ Myself, Cindy- 8 years old.

"I'll do the feeding!" yelled Jessica.

"I'll wash the dog," Dominique said.

"I'll train it," followed Darryl.

"I'll play with it," I said.

"Me, too. Me, too. Can we play with it, too?" asked Corina and Corey.

"Alright. Alright. How about we all play with it?" I suggested.

"We forgot to talk about what we're going to do before the puppy gets here," I told them.

"And we forgot to think about a name for it," said Jessica.

"How about if we name it Mikki?" I said.

"Why Mikki? asked Jessica.

"I think it's okay," Darryl said, favoring with me. "It's a new name."

"Yeah! Let's call it Mikki," yelled Corina and Corey.

"Little Mike? Jessica? Dominique?" I said, waiting for an answer.

"Hey, it's fine with me," answered Little Mike with a smirk on his face. "It sounds like my name."

Little Mike was standing behind Jessica. He was so tiny, I could hardly see him.

"Well, alright," said Dominique.

"I like it," Jessica answered.

"Mikki it is," Darryl said with a smile on his face. "Yes! Tomorrow Mikki will be with us."

Chapter 2

Finally, the big day arrived. It was a Saturday. Papa left the house at exactly eleven o'clock a.m.

We were all in the backyard, except for Little Mike.

"We have to set up everything before Mikki gets here," I said.

"Hey, I'm here!" Little Mike shouted. He opened the backyard gate and came in.

"Let's go check out what's in the doggy bag," I said.

"Where's the doggy bag?" Darryl asked.

"Yeah, where's the doggy back?" asked Corina with curiosity.

"Not doggy back," I laughed. "It's doggy bag."

"It's a bag with stuff in it for the puppy."

"I heard Dad say yesterday that he put all the stuff the dog needs in a plastic bag in the kitchen closet," Dominique said.

Everyone raced toward the kitchen.

We opened the closet and found the bag on the floor. It had two big bags of dog food, a few bags of treats, one blue and one red plastic bowl, a plastic bottle of dog shampoo, a brown brush, a blue dog leash, and some dog toys.

Papa had bought a beautiful and big doghouse. It was gray, with a green roof and two windows.

7

We took all the toys out of the bag and put them in the doghouse.

Then, we put some water in one of the bowls, some food in the other bowl, and put them inside the doghouse, too.

"Yeah, we did it! We did it all for Mikki!" Dominique shouted.

Later, someone came into the house. It was Papa.

Chapter 3

Everyone raced inside to meet Mikki. "Where is it? Where is Mikki?"

Before we reached where Papa was standing, a beautiful, hairy, black and brown puppy jumped up in the air and wagged its tail.

It headed toward us, then started sniffing and licking all of us.

It was a big puppy.

It jumped on Corey and almost dropped him to the floor.

"Looks like he's happy to meet his new friends," Papa said.

We were fighting to pick Mikki up.

Papa stood there looking at us with a big smile on his face.

Corina and Corey started whining like little cry babies.

"Okay, why don't you kids take turns? Mikki is everybody's puppy," Papa reminded us.

"How about we let the younger kids go first?"

"Just go first, you big babies," Dominique said.

"We'll get to play with Mikki longer than you guys anyway," Darryl said. "We're older."

We each got a chance to pet Mikki. Then, we asked Papa if we could bring him to the back-yard and play with him.

We let Mikki walk alongside us with his tail still wagging. He was having a lot of fun jumping around and darting in and out between our legs.

Mikki was happy to see his doghouse. He went inside it and started biting on all the toys and kicking the food bowls all over the place.

Mikki made us happy that day. Papa was chuckling.

Some days Mikki made us happy.
Some days he made us mad.
Some days Mikki made us worry.
Some days he made us sad.
One big day, he surprised us.

Chapter 4

Nikki made us mad the day he ate Papa's donuts.

At the time, Papa was downstairs talking to Little Mike's dad, Mr. Williams.

Momma was back from the grocery store.

We helped her put the groceries away and went to Darryl's bedroom to play video games.

Later, we heard Momma and Papa speaking very loud. Then, the playroom door flew open.

They both stood there looking at us. Papa looked upset and Momma had her hands on her waist.

"Okay, spill the beans," Momma said. "Who ate the donuts?"

We looked at each other, wondering what had happened.

"What happened, Momma?" Darryl asked.

"Yeah, what happened?" asked Dominique.

"The box of donuts I bought for your father is on the counter empty. Which one of you did it?"

"We don't know what you're talking about," I said.

"We've been playing video games since we helped Momma put away the groceries."

"It wasn't me or your father. You kids have been together. Someone had to eat them," Momma said.

"I'm giving you guys two minutes to tell me who ate my donuts," said Papa in an angry tone. "Darryl, I know you will tell me who did it."

"For real, Dad, we didn't do it," Darryl answered.

Momma and Papa left the room. We followed them and headed for the kitchen. We wanted to find out what happened to the donuts.

The donut box was still on the counter, but torn. Inside, there was only one chocolate donut left.

Chapter 5

I spotted some sprinkles of crumbs and white powder on the floor.

Suddenly, I thought of something.

"Oh, no!" I shouted. "Mikki!"

Mikki had been quiet the entire time. We thought he was sleeping.

Papa looked at one corner of the kitchen and spotted him.

He was crouching, his face full of white powder, crumbs all around him, and his stomach blown up like a balloon.

Everyone was laughing, except Papa. He didn't think it was funny.

"Come on, Bob, it's not all that bad," Momma said.

"After all, he did leave you one. A chocolate one," she continued as she laughed."

"That's not funny," Papa said to Momma.

He then turned around and looked at Mikki. "You're on punishment, Mister."

"Oh, Daddy, poor Mikki," said Dominique. "You're making him feel bad."

We then took Mikki into Darryl's bedroom with us.

We kept him away from Papa for a few days.

Chapter 6

Mikki made us worry one morning, when we saw a cut on his head while he was sleeping in his doghouse.

No one knew what happened. We began looking for clues in the backyard.

"Daddy, look," Darryl said, pointing at the backyard fence.

Papa looked at the fence and saw a hole in the dirt under it.

"Oh, boy," I heard Papa say. "I think I know

what happened. It looks like Mikki snuck out last night."

Papa cleaned the cut with a wet cotton ball. He then put a band-aid on it to protect Mikki's forehead.

Later, he put some dirt in the hole under the fence.

The next night, I heard a strange sound coming from the backyard. I looked and saw Mikki running toward the house with a bunch of other dogs.

Dominique was sleeping in the other bed next to the door.

"Dominique! Dominique!" I shouted. "Wake up! You have to see this."

"What? I don't want to eat now," she mumbled.

Dominique often talked in her sleep.

"Dominique! Wake up! Look outside! It's Mikki!"

Dominique finally jumped out of her bed and went to the window.

We both saw Mikki squeezing under the fence Papa had just fixed. Then, he went into his house.

"Now we know what's been going on," Dominique said.

The next day, we told Papa about what we saw.

This time, he put some wire at the bottom of the fence. The wire went all the way inside the dirt.

Mikki kept digging deeper into the dirt and leaving-But, he always came back before we woke up.

Chapter 7

Mikki made us sad the day papa took him for a walk.

That day it was drizzling. Mikki saw another dog across the street and pulled away from Papa's hand. He chased the dog down the street.

Papa chased after him, yelling his name. Mikki kept running and running. He didn't go back to Papa.

After Papa told us the sad news, we decided we had to do everything we could to find Mikki.

We drove around our neighborhood and other neighborhoods. We went to the dog pound and many animal shelters. We handed out flyers with Mikki's picture on them.

We couldn't find Mikki.

Everyday, we waited and waited. Mikki never came back come.

"Is Mikki coming back, Mom?" Darryl asked Momma.

"I don't know, D," Momma answered.

"Don't worry, kids," Papa said. "I promise I will get you another dog."

"We don't want another dog. We want Mikki," Darryl said with his eyes tearing.

Day and night we talked about Mikki. We laughed about all the fun things he used to do.

Since Mikki didn't come back, we put all his toys and food bowls away, inside his dog house.

However, every night, I kept looking outside of my bedroom window. I was hoping he would show up someday.

Chapter 8

Since we didn't want to stay sad for ever, we agreed to get another pet.

It wasn't going to be another dog. We didn't want to replace Mikki.

Soon after, Papa took us to the pet shop.

We bought a beautiful and brightly colored yellow and green parrot, and a brown cat with white stripes.

We named the parrot, Harryl, and the cat, Tigress.

Tigress's stripes made her look like a baby tiger.

Darryl chose the name Harryl because it sounded like his name.

Darryl and Harryl became best friends.

Harryl stayed in his cage right next to Darryl's bed. He also woke him up every morning.

"Good morning. Good morning."

Darryl said he liked it when Harryl woke him up. That helped him to get up on time.

We only allowed Tigress in Darryl's bedroom when I was there to hold her and keep her from going next to Harryl's cage.

She enjoyed purring and lying on my lap.

Momma bought her a blue yarn ball. She enjoyed running around the house chasing it.

Tigress and Harryl were fun, but we still missed Mikki.

We thought we would never see him again, until…

Chapter 9

One day, Papa spotted a dog that looked just like Mikki.

This happened somewhere far from home.

The dog was standing next to an old man sitting on a chair.

Papa pulled down the window and called out Mikki's name.

The dog ran to him and jumped on the car floor with its tail wagging.

30

Papa knew it was Mikki. The scar from the cut was still on his forehead.

Papa took the dog back to the old man.

"Good afternoon, dear Sir."

"Well, good afternoon, Sir. Is there sumthin' can help you with?"

"Yes, Sir. My name is Mr. Robert Thomas."

"Well, I am Mr. Gullerfiddle."

The old man spoke in a funny manner.

"Your dog looks just like our lost puppy."

"Well, this is Flipsy, my new companion," Mr. Gullerfiddle said.

"Well, you see, one morning I heard sumthin' scratching at my door."

"Well, I got up to see what it was."

"Well, when I opened the door, a dog ran inside the house."

31

"Well, the dog was dirty and it was shaking. I washed it and fed it."

"Well, it never left my side since that day."

"What happened to his collar?" asked Papa.

"Well, you see, he didn't have one on when he first came here."

"Well, Sir, if you want him back, you can have him back," Mr. Gullerfiddle continued.

"I sure will miss him, though. I ain't got no family or friends."

"We'll see," Papa answered. I'll go home and ask the kids what they think."

Later, Papa came home to share the big news.

Chapter 10

That was the day *Mikki surprised us.*

Papa told us Mikki had a new owner and a new name.

"Why didn't you bring him home with you, Dad?" asked Darryl.

"Well, I'll take you guys to see him," Papa answered. "Then, we'll decide what to do."

On our way, we spotted Little Mike walking out of his house."

"Can Little Mike come with us, Dad?" asked Darryl.

"Sure," Papa answered.

"We found Mikki!" we all shouted as soon as Little Mike opened the car door.

"What!!? Who!!? Mikki!!? Where is he?" he asked.

"Daddy's taking us now to see him," I said.

When we arrived, Papa knocked at Mr. Gullerfiddle's door.

"Well, hello again Mr. Thomas. Are these Flipsy's old friends?"

"Kids, say hello to Mr. Gullerfiddle," Papa said.

"Hello, Mr. Gubblefibble. I'm Cindy."

"Hello, I'm Darryl."

"Me, I'm Dominique."

"And, I'm Little Mike."

"Well, it's a pleasure to meet y'all," Mr. Gullerfiddle answered.

Meanwhile, we heard a dog barking from inside the house. Mr. Gullerfiddle opened the door wider, and the dog came running out.

Then, it started sniffing and licking us. Mikki used to do those same things.

The only difference was that dog looked much bigger than Mikki.

"We missed you, Mikki," Little Mike and Darryl said.

We hugged Mikki. We didn't want to let him go.

"Kids, we have to make a decision," Papa reminded us.

"Should we take Mikki back? Or, should we leave him with Mr. Gullerfiddle?"

"I miss Mikki. I want him back," I said.

"I want Mikki back," Dominique cried.

"Mr. Gullenbiddle looks sad," said Darryl. He will miss Mikki very much."

"Yeah…but, Mikki wants to go back home with us," I added.

Chapter 11

Little Mike didn't say anything. However, he looked sad.

All of a sudden, Mikki turned around and headed back toward Mr. Gullerfiddle's door with his tail wagging.

We called out his name, but he didn't come back.

"Well, kids, it looks like Mikki has made his choice," Papa said.

"Besides, Mr. Gullerfiddle needs him more than we do."

"Well, thank you very much, good people," said Mr. Gullerfiddle when Papa told him our decision.

"Flipsy is very happy here," he continued. "Well, I feed him, I wash him, and I play with him."

"I take good care of him. He's my best friend."

"Bye, Mikki."

"Bye, Mikki."

"We'll miss you."

We waved good-bye to Mr. Gullerfiddle and to Mikki. Mikki stood right next to his new owner. His tongue was hanging and his tail was still wagging.

"Will Mr. Gubblelubble be good to Mikki, addy?" asked Dominique.

"Sure, he will, pudding."

"His name is Mr. Gullerfiddle, not ubblebubble," Papa laughed.

"I'll call him too, sometimes, to find out if likki is okay."

"Can we go visit Mikki again?" asked Darryl.

"Sure, we can," Papa replied with a smile.

We finally arrived back home.

"I found Mikki. I found Mikki," Harryl elled.

"Where's Mikki?" Momma asked.

"He stayed with Mr. Gullerfiddle, his new wner" I answered.

"Mikki don't like us no more," said ominique in a baby tone.

41

"Let's just say Mikki made the decision," Papa said.

"He chose to stay with his new friend."

"What's more important is that he's happy."

"Let's go finish the game, guys," Darryl said

"I bet I'll beat you this time," I teased him.

We ran into Darryl's bedroom. Tigress followed us.

She jumped up onto my laps and laid her head there.

We're happy to have Tigress and Harryl as our new pets.

However, we will never forget Mikki.

As Papa said, what's important now is that he's happy and we can see him again.